"Pia's poems capture echoes from the past, reflections on the present and hope for the future. T.S. Eliot in "Four Quartets" writes:

> "Footfalls echo in the memory
> Down the passage that we did not take
> Towards the door we never opened
> Into the rose-garden"

The echoes from Pia's life as she reflects on the harsh realities of life's experiences and the disappointment of unfulfilled dreams can evoke our own echoes. But her poetry does more than dwell on life's disappointments; it also reveals the healing power of beauty glimpsed in nature and in life-affirming relationships. She moves from darkness to light; from despair to discovery and to the assured hope of the eternal "Rose Garden".

Robyn Claydon
Author/International speaker/Lecturer in Poetry/
Listed in the World's Who's Who of Women and the
Dictionary of Distinguished Leadership

"Great poems and perfect synesthesia (words and art)."

Koraljka
Artist and Illustrator

"I have found Pia's "Spirituality" poetry to be consistent and life giving and I commend the work highly.

Her poems are almost Psalm-ic or Proverbial in the biblical sense. They often present a 'tension' which needs resolution, which comes to finalization in the last stanza, bringing release and joy.

I consider this to be a valuable piece of work and I thank her for allowing me the privilege of critique."

Ralph Estherby
Author/Australian Army Chaplain/Director of Chaplaincy Australia/
Senior Pastor at Breakthrough (ACC) Church Hornsby

MY BEST POEMS

Part 3

SPIRITUALITY

Finding the way out of the maze

© 2017 by Pia Horan-Gross

All rights reserved. No portion of this book may be reproduced, stored in a retrieval system, or transmitted in any form or by any means – electronic, mechanical, photocopy, recording, scanning, or other – except for brief quotations in critical reviews or articles, without the prior written permission of the author/self-publisher.

Unless otherwise noted, Scripture quotations are taken form the Holy Bible, New King James Version (NKJV)®. Copyright © 1982 by Thomas Nelson. Used by permission. All rights reserved.

ISBN 978-0-6480135-3-2

Table of Contents

FOREWORD	ix
A PICTURE OF THE VINEYARD	1
ABIDING	3
ANCIENT MANUSCRIPTS DECLARE	4
BLEAK DAY	6
BLESSED	8
CAGES	9
CESSPOOL	11
CHAMELEON	13
COCOON	15
CONSTRICTION	17
CONTEMPLATING MORTALITY	18
CORRIDORS	21
COUNT BLUEBEARD	22
COVERINGS	24
DRIFTING	25
EASTER REFLECTIONS	26
EX NIHILE	28
EXPRESSING THE INEXPRESSIBLE	30
FAITH vs. EXPECTATIONS	32
FAITH	34
FIG LEAVES	36

FREE TO LOVE	37
GENESIS AGAIN	38
GOD'S RICHNESS	40
HAY AND STUBBLE	41
HE KNOWS	42
HIS GIFT	44
HIS TEMPLE	47
HOUSE OF MIRRORS	48
IN HIM	50
IN HIS SAFE KEEPING – AT LAST!	51
LIFE'S LEARNING	52
LIFE'S LINK	53
MIRRORS	54
MY BELOVED	56
MY SWITZERLAND	57
NECESSARY DISILLUSIONMENT	58
NEW WORLD	60
ON MY WAY TO WORK	62
OUR MAGNIFICENT DESTINY	64
PARADISE	65
PRAYER	67
PRISONS	68
RESTLESS	69
RISEN	70

SCAPEGOAT	71
SEA OF TEARS	73
SHELTER FROM THE STORM	75
SHUTDOWN	76
SIMPLICITY	78
SURVIVAL DEMANDS IT	79
THE ALTAR OF THE LIE	81
THE ARTFUL DODGER	83
THE DAM	84
THE FINAL VERDICT	85
THE GOLDEN CUP OF POISON	87
THE GREAT WEDDING FEAST	89
THE GREATEST GIFT OF ALL	90
THE IDEALIST	92
THE MEANING OF LIFE	94
THE MYTH OF SELF-SUFFICIENCY	96
THE ONE ESSENTIAL THING	98
THE PARABLE OF FIRE	100
THE RELIGIOUS SELF	102
THE TEMPLE	103
THE UNIVERSAL FOUNT	106
TIME ALONE	108
WAKING FROM STUPOR	109
AUTHOR WEBSITE DETAILS	111

FOREWORD

Psalm 73:26 "My body and mind may waste away, but God remains the foundation of my life and my inheritance forever." (GOD'S WORD® Translation)

The sub-title of this book of poetry summarizes my life experience and the above Scripture confirms it. My heart often failed and still fails me at times but my spirit is daily growing stronger.

I hope you, dear reader, will find this booklet refreshing, both to mind and body and strengthening to your spirit. I believe it speaks to people of all ages and walks of life. My aim and delight is to instill hope to the weary and increased courage, in order to face this thing called life.

None of us have chosen to be put on this earth but as we are now here, we may as well make the most of it by investing our time and focus wisely. You may be sitting in a prison cell, or some other kind of prison, or living it up (bored maybe of it?); the time is now! My struggles have been many but once, at rock bottom, I remember saying to myself: "It can only go up from here on!" and living it as if I meant it!

The greatest surprise for me has been to discover that the whole universe is permeated by a benevolent, yet powerful Spirit, who is eager to be found and to help us become the best we can be! This is a hidden truth, discovered mainly on a personal level, although by countless millions already. Evil is of course what is most apparent in our world.

At the back of this book you will find my author website details.
I would love to hear how my book has impacted you.

A PICTURE OF THE VINEYARD

I saw a vineyard
at the time of harvest.
The vines were at their best,
heavy with big succulent grapes.
Their bowing branches
secured with man-made supports.

The vineyard was a picture of
perfection. Green leaves, in beautiful
contrast with round, deep purple grapes,
against a background of azure sky,
sprinkled with white fluffy clouds.
The world could stand still now!

Then came the harvesters,
cutting off the precious clusters,
gathering them in large baskets
and bringing them to the pressing vats.
The air filled with singing
and excitement at the good yield.

I became dismayed,
as the vine was gradually stripped
of its precious and beautiful yearly harvest.
So much patience producing that glorious fruit!
Glad of the outcome,
yet sad at the ensuing devastation.

Then the shocking realization
that the perfectly formed fruit,
lovingly tended by sun, rain
and human hands,
was to be crushed
into an awful pungent paste!

The Owner of the vineyard
is not aiming for the fruit itself.
He has a different purpose in mind.
In order to achieve the excellence of wine,
the fruit needs to be transformed,
by becoming a living sacrifice.

3 September 2005

ABIDING

Show me Lord
how to keep a soft heart,
without breaking my heart.

Show me Lord
how to keep a soft heart,
without hardening my heart,
as a defense.

Show me Lord
How, with this soft heart,
not to hold onto pain
until it brings forth death,
in the fruit of gloom.

Aware of people's hearts-
your response,
neither hardness nor gloom.
Instead, love and compassion,
while abiding in the Father;
your own heart resting safe and secure.

Show me Lord,
how to keep a soft heart-
by abiding in You.

Early 1980's

ANCIENT MANUSCRIPTS DECLARE

Ancient manuscripts declare:
The One who put together
flesh and bones,
nerves and sinews,
brain and mind,
heart and soul;
who skillfully weaved the DNA,
each strand to form a different chain;
who established the chemistry of cells
and commissioned legions of T- soldiers,
putting to shame man's awkward attempts
at guarding homeostasis' original design;
this One, the ancients say,
not only excels in knowledge and wisdom;
He also has a passionate heart for all He created,
which He guards jealously!
Fully understanding and committed
to His creation's needs,
He is Lord, without lording it over them.
Rather, He wants to be known
as Abba, a tender, loving parent.
Showing, through nature-
one of his clearest tools-
just how much He cares.

Doting mother hen and her chicks,
and the fierceness of a mother bear with cubs,
to name just a few.
Most importantly,
Jesus Christ, His only Son,
on the cross.
Is it too hard then, to respond to Him
in wonder and simple adoration?

30 January 2010

BLEAK DAY

Silent walking
on a cold, bleak day.
Hands in my pockets,
collar rolled up.
Rainclouds racing,
grey ripples on the lake.
Bare trees,
their leaves
strewn across my path.

Memories
of a similar scene-
aimlessly searching
for the unknown.
Lost and driven,
tightness within.
Questioning,
was there a hiding place
from that dull inner ache?
Much to think about,
so few answers!
The usual conclusion:
keep walking...
I am still walking-
in wonder now.

16 December 2006
Greenwell Point, NSW

BLESSED

Lord, where are you? he cried.
I am desperate.
Where are you?
All he could see,
through the tears,
were the infinite starry skies.
So remote and cold.

Why are you silent
when I need you most?
Blind, these eyes! he thought,
for I cannot see Him.
Neither can I touch Him,
nor hear Him.
What a useless body!

Then: Lord,
it's all too hard.
I need to touch,
hear and
see you tonight!
After a while-
silent resignation.

It was then that he heard
a timeless, tender voice,
by-passing his natural senses.
A word spoken into his spirit.
"Blessed are those
who have not seen
and yet believe." (John 20:29)
    (In memory of an actual event
        in 1984)

CAGES

The world's cages,
locked within cages.
Attempts to escape
and promises of liberty, at best,
only ever change the cage.

All in cages
many don't see.
False beliefs blinding
glimmers of freedom.
Promises only ever partly fulfilled.

One cage treatment,
another sobriety,
try correction and probation.
If these don't work,
simply change your identity.

Entertainment and fun
are more subtle than all
but dump you the quickest.
Soon you find yourself
back in your cage.

The world continues spinning-
the cages rattle and squeak.
Discarded, golden keys of broken promises,
glistening in an arctic sun.
Piercing, the world's primeval scream.

End the poem here?
Revel in hopeless despair?
More real, maybe?
Or more artistic that way?
So some would say!

I will frustrate
morose reality
and proudly state:
There is a counterpart
to human despair!

A master key
that opens all the locks.
Not shiny, nor golden,
but wooden, bloodstained
and in the form of a cross.

Written in 1992

CESSPOOL

Man's world-
a cesspool
of unrelenting chaos.
Man's will- jostling for control.
Man's thoughts-
messages in a bottle,
drifting on storm tossed seas.
Man's hunger-
big fish eating little ones.
Power and its pursuit
swallows up the one seeking it.
Those who find themselves
trusted leaders in the midst of all this,
easily become caught
in the quicksand of controversy.
The world would have you believe
that it is all about self!
The seas have become too small
for all those clamouring for a catch.
The truth isn't heard in the storm
nor in the frantic pace of life.
It requires drawing aside,
finding your own island,
returning to it often and persistently.
Becoming attuned
to that still small voice,
devoid of seduction or flattery.

The One who knows us as we are
welcomes us,
bringing refreshing and cleansing
and reminding us,
to our great relief,
that it is all about Him and His ways.
This is to be our focus,
our anchor,
as we seek to serve Him,
in His name,
in the cesspool of a drifting world.

10 September 2013

CHAMELEON

Through practice and necessity,
the chameleon has learned to mimic
every variation of its surroundings.
A master at concealment,
does it care about its true identity?

Its adaptation to stick and stone
and the in-built capacity to change its hue;
fascinating and puzzling indeed!
The underlying reasons;
protection and to fool its prey.

Among humans, a counterpart;
those that deftly project
what self-interest would demand.
Adapting their words and deeds
to what cunning dictates.

Some, like chameleon,
do it unawares;
a learned response
they picked up early in life,
like puppets on a string.

You find these chameleons
in every sphere of life,
piously sitting in church pews,
or else running big corporations,
charm a common disguise.

Do they care about their true identity?
Do they ever ask themselves:
what am I really here for,
apart from looking out for number one?
What bliss to find that God-given true self!

Written approx. 1979
(re-written 2016)

COCOON

(Joshua 5:13-15)

Inside this cocoon,
cozy and safe,
at times
the urge,
even need
to move my wings.
Mostly though,
comfortable
to just stay put.

Lately,
restlessness
and dissatisfaction,
living in the cocoon.
Dreaming of sailing
under stormy skies,
driven by strong currents,
daring to face
unknown dangers.

Longing to join brave hearts,
engaged in this holy war;
to release captives,
dying in their cocoons,
as well as wounded prey.
To be part of the holy assembly,
gathered around the Great Captain.
To become acquainted with His battle plans,
equipped with His armour and weapons of war.

I will continue breaking
out. Comfort now a prison.
On and on
this dream is driving me.
Little by little,
the walls are giving way.
The risk of what may be
and dangers assured:
a price I am willing to pay.

7 December 2001

CONSTRICTION

Over the years,
a shriveling,
a constriction of the heart.
The hand once opened
has tightened its grip.
Instead of scattering seeds,
careful additions and subtractions.
The ardour of dreams,
given way
to dull compromise.
Soberness regarding self
and others,
mingled with short bursts of panic,
camouflaged behind a veil of busyness.
Experience has added skills
in the art of appearances
and deepened isolation.
So many comforts needed
to silence the crying heart!
Turning away from self,
hope is found
or rediscovered.
By opening one's heart,
just a little,
one steps into the road to life.

30 December 1993

CONTEMPLATING MORTALITY

Tear-filled waves of mortality
sweeping over me.
What appeared a challenge,
now a mere reminder of struggle
and increasing frailty.
A need to come away and reflect,
to process the shifting reality
of life's present stage.
For a time,
to contemplate a broken past.
What to keep and treasure?
What to let go,
to wrap in grave shroud and to bury?
Only then,
to direct my gaze
to what lies ahead.

Fleeing for a while
from self-imposed demands,
and needs for constant care.
To-do lists, my daily diet
(a daily obsession?).
Presently, I look around me–
this little caravan, once a delight.
Like me now,
showing signs of wear and tear.
Ants have taken up residence,
letting me know- I don't belong!

A spider weaved its web
in a new gap of the broken seal,
letting the rain in;
leaving behind stains and mould.
Decay setting in here too...

It seems that I have bitten off
more than I can chew.
A residue of past irresponsibility,
due to a then inability
to rightly assess situations,
people,
strengths and weaknesses
and making decisions accordingly.
Pain dealt with,
by substituting it
with a virtual world,
which tended to jar
with what was.
All reinforcing the habit
of living in unreality.
Eventually, tired of living a lie.

Now a thought, as quick as a flash:
"what gives value to my present life"?
"The people who allow me to love them?"
A still small voice within adds:
"Not just those you choose
but also those I send to you."
This is the new challenge:
not trying to prove anything.
A death knell to womanly bravado!

Just a niggling, yet liberating request
to live the life He has called me to,
though previously, amply proven a failure,
except to do it, moment by moment,
by faith in His enabling Love.
My weakness, frailty and mortality
now surrendered to His strength.

Wyee Point, NSW
10 November 2014

CORRIDORS

locked doors
empty corridors
walls white
shiny and sterile
hollow screams

words
echoing
towering
barricading
imploding

on a door
Love
and
No Admission
Need, not the password

the robot hand of loneliness
monotonously
and repetitive
reaches out-
you're back in your cell

4 October 1981

COUNT BLUEBEARD

Once again,
I have turned the key
to that forbidden room.

Anew,
staring
upon bloody, severed heads.

Despite myself,
becoming an accomplice
in the heinous deeds of rage.

This time,
I made a pact
with the One who keeps vigil.

Preceding-
fearless and honest confession
of violent words.

In future,
refraining
from entering Bluebeard's domain.

In times of pressure,
running to the Guardian
instead. The key- in His
safekeeping!

12 March 2005

COVERINGS

Humans
find it very difficult
to acknowledge nakedness,
especially before our Creator.

Like those first parents,
we rush to cover ourselves
with man-made coverings-
inadequate at best.

Endless disputes continue,
igniting countless wars.
Inter-personal
and pandemic blame abounds.

That false covering-
originating in pride,
hiding toxic shame,
in order to present whole.

The lie acknowledged:
one step towards true wisdom.
Offered instead, is an adequate Covering,
ensuring true and lasting peace.

30 January 2016

DRIFTING

Strange and eerie-
a ship that's lost direction;
drifting
in the midst of the sea,
tossed about
by wind and waves.

Imperfect and frail,
any sense of self gone,
with no going back.
Bridges burned.
The future
uncertain and bleak.

Excitement for new things
vainly pursued.
Past hopes-
a smoldering pile of ashes.
Exhortations and pep-talks-
too hollow to hear.

Though rudderless,
on an ocean of lost dreams;
nevertheless,
my vessel is sailing
firm and secure,
in the palm of His hand!

March 1993

EASTER REFLECTIONS

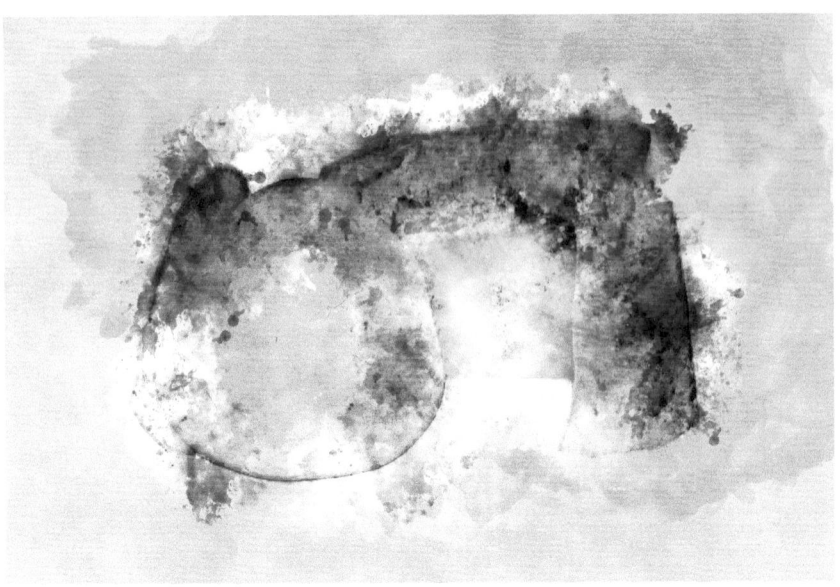

He loved us completely,
offering the ultimate price.
No seeming guarantee then
it would ever pay off.
Love driven by love.
Recklessly, risking His very all,
for love's sake.

A free act,
springing from a free choice.
Yet, also a response
to the call of the Father.
Proving that His will
is highly desirable-
its outcome worth dying for.

Looking briefly into the abyss of fear- then
exchanging fear with trust.
By committing Himself into the Father's
care, surrendering all personal power,
He released the miracle of resurrection.
His victory- inspiring millions to rise up and,
in His name, to love recklessly.

                                                         18 September
                                                         2003

EX NIHILO

This morning
on waking,
out of the blue,
the thought,
or rather
the question
arose:
Why
is the earth,
in its center,
a ball of fire?

Why
create it such?
I am struck,
once again,
at the wonder
of this Mind
who created our world
and the worlds
so perfect,
without a prototype,
rather– ex nihilo!

What a mind!
What a being!
Could one put together
all the wisdom of man,
in comparison,
it would be a mere drop
in the oceans of the world.

My reflection went further.
This incredible being
delights in being called Father,
by those who love Him.

He has prepared a kingdom,
a place for many to dwell,
walking and talking together with Him ,
in the cool of gardens of delight.
The only condition:
no contamination, through sin, to enter in.
Instead,
cleansing confession and baptism in water,
bowing to the kingship of His Son,
and only then to enter through the Door,
appointed by Him. (John 10:9)

21 November 2007

EXPRESSING THE INEXPRESSIBLE

Contemplating from my window
the new wonder of a sunrise,
amid the call of the Currawong,
I become aware once more-

You are my first impulse
to greet You,
each day
when I regain waking consciousness.

You are the sunlight that pierces through,
gradually dispelling the heaviness,
when in me
I discover a foggy greyness.

You are the Majestic Artist
who, ex nihilo, long ago
created goodness and beauty
and every day anew.

You remain in control
amidst seeming chaos and despair-
the eye of the storm
dwells in perfect calm.

You are the lofty One, the One enthroned.
The self-sufficient One.
Through Calvary,
wooing Your creation back to Yourself.

You are the One
Who freely chose to tie Yourself
with an everlasting oath, a covenant,
to the shiftiness of the human heart- my heart!

July 1994

FAITH vs. EXPECTATIONS

Today,
the sting of disappointment,
once again.

An outcome hoped for
perished and died,
once again.

What did I place my faith in?
Favourable circumstances,
once again?

Or was it in a certain outcome
involving a specific person,
once again?

Fickle human hope,
versus faith in something unshakable,
once again?

It is staggering to me;
the persistence of the same mistake,
once again!

Faulty thinking plaguing this representative
of the human race,
once again.

I awaken to the fact
that I am called to faith,
once again.

Somehow,
the penny doesn't seem to drop,
once again.

The concept of faith confused
with fickle, soulish expectations,
once again.

When the latter get dashed,
disappointment tries to steal even my faith,
once again.

I need the dividing scalpel of the Word;
A lie-ectomy of heart and mind,
once again.

Once removed and put on the altar,
God's consuming fire will deal with it –
once and for all!

17 February 2016

FAITH

Faith, like love-
usually misunderstood.
When spoken of,
one's own version perceived.

The faithful-
those
who together
uphold a common creed?

From mere observation,
while comfortable in safe detachment,
trembling, I took a leap...
of faith!

That very faith-
through and in the One,
opened a door to His Realm.
Newfound, all of Heaven's resources!

There is an age-old counterfeit,
weaving through fables,
myths and the occult,
promising power: dark and self-serving.

True faith,
given in order to love
and to do His will on earth-
part of our magnificent destiny!

Yet, even among those
said to have "ears to hear",
often an impotent understanding.
Birds that never leave their nests.

Surrounded by the earthbound,
it is risky to start flapping one's wings.
Our fragile egos bruised
by the consequences of practice.

Faith never guarantees instant success.
But act we must!
We have sure promises
from One who cannot lie.

12 July 2010

FIG LEAVES

Why insist
on wearing fig leaves,
when Father prepared
a covering, costly indeed?
It provides warmth,
beauty and restoration.
A covering for shame,
an invitation to the humble
to belong.

Instead,
we revel in our self-adequacy,
pouring contempt on dependence.
We point the finger
at the glaring faults of others
blind to see them in ourselves,
while failing to see
three more fingers
pointing back at us!

2 November 2007

FREE TO LOVE

Lord,
if there is one prayer
I pray above all else
it is this-
to be set free
from the tyranny
of my own needs,
the self-centeredness
of my petty frustrations,
the endless array
of wants and cravings-
in order to love
the unlovable,
like me.

To find the caring,
the courage,
the challenge,
in order to embrace
the broken-hearted-
despite my ripped out heart.
To focus instead
on hope and faith,
and to learn to trust You.
No longer
tossed to and fro,
due to fickleness.
LORD set me free
to love as You love me!

(Undated)

GENESIS AGAIN

"The earth was without form, and void,
and darkness was on the face of the deep.
And the Spirit of God was hovering
Over the face of the waters." (Genesis 1:2)

Plunged in darkness,
roaring arctic winds
sweep over earth's surface.
The howling spirit of the world
whipping up waves,
crowned with black foam.

Earth's positioning in the universe
to receive life from the sun
and steady watering from its ecosystem-
not yet in place.
Oversight by a skilled manager-
not yet fashioned from the earth.

Many unknown millenniums from there,
darkness once again covering the earth.
This time, due to the enemy's workings
and his successful takeover bid;
man, sacked from his job-
a hobo, sifting through the world's trash.

A rescue plan devised from the start,
despite the deepening darkness
of centuries of failure and sin.
The golden thread of a promise,
confirmed by prophets: God's Calvary.
Confounding to all.

That insignificant-looking shoot,
springing forth from a long-felled stump,
accomplished that second Genesis of man.
Darkness swallowed by the Light of the World.
The sure promise of walks anew,
in the cool of His gardens of delight.

30 November 2000

GOD'S RICHNESS

Manifold wisdom,
uncontainable,
past human comprehension.
As high as the sky is above the earth,
so high are His ways.
Only a fraction revealed,
reflected in creation.
Innumerable manifestations
of beauty and perfection,
evoking worship.
Unlimited generosity, freely shared.

Extravagant lover for love's sake.
Your arms are never full.
Countless, your thoughts towards us.
The treasury of your gifts- never exhausted.
Eternity barely contains
all that you have in store for us.
You delight to delight
and to enlarge the joyful giver-
to make room for the lonely.
You take the willing heart,
to reflect your own.

26 July 2012

HAY AND STUBBLE

Many words,
mere hype.
The greater the shallowness,
the louder the noise.

Wordiness,
to cover up lack.
Decorative words,
like peacock feathers.

Unless words
match actions
and actions
match words...

Mere sound waves,
tickling some ears.
Like rainless clouds;
hunger and thirst left untouched.

Words He calls
hay and stubble.
Destined
for the fire of His judgement.

August 1994

HE KNOWS

(Isaiah 49:2)

Presently,
in limbo.
Sharp pain arising
from the distant memory
of taking wings.

Living
in chosen confinement,
minimal space
and limited tasks-
the rigidity of discipline.

Apparently, the fastest,
most accurate arrows
are made from twisted,
gnarled and tortured
desert wood.

Drenched,
stretched,
methodically pinned down,
until finally
the end goal is reached.

Before,
seemingly useless
to the untrained eye.
Now, made dead straight
and excelling in springiness.

Knowing the Master's ways,
takes away quiet despair.
He is well acquainted
with my desire to fly,
his greater purpose I will trust.

Middle Pocket, NSW
16 August 1984

HIS GIFT

Days of relaxed pondering,
sensing His constant presence.
My van parked amidst empty sites.
Wind gusts in the trees, then pouring rain.
Soon, the blazing sun returns,
shadowed by intermittent racing clouds.
On weekends, the sites fill up:
families with kids,
noisily populating pools
and jumping atop rubber mounds.
Fishermen sitting around at night,
a little too jolly for sobriety.

My aloneness now a heavy garment,
conscious of it when I gaze out to sea,
watching bold surfers,
like corks in the distance.
A black dog, a friendly mutt,
racing up and down the beach.

He runs up to people,
while looking out concerned,
his master disappearing under waves.
Now near me, shaking himself, shivering,
turning around and whimpering,
cold from vainly joining his owner-

The weight is there too,
when walking along the beach;
a mum watching her kids playing
near the edge of the sea,
an animated group of friends
walking past me.

I look for treasures cast up by the sea,
quietly praying for a sign
of His constant presence.
A bright blue stone maybe?
A definite rarity
and worthy love token!

Yet, proofs of His love
already more than a few-
and I am chastened.
The next day I follow a path
around the Peninsula,
to the river's mouth.

Many smooth, multi-coloured stones
along its rocky shore.
A blue one?
I find blue chips,
fragments of shells,
but no blue stone.

Then-
a bright red coral catches my eye!
I bend down and pick it up;
although a-symmetric,
like the human heart,
that is exactly its shape!

Sculpted by a loving
yet invisible hand;
His tools:
sand, rocks, turbulent waters
and time.
My heart and spirit now singing!

27 November 2011
Crookhaven Heads

HIS TEMPLE

With a whip of cords,
He drives them all out.
"Take these things away!"
The Temple is His Body,
not built with human hands;
its building stones
made up by those
sealed with His Spirit.
Should the idols of sloth and
greed, lust and pride therefore
co-habit with His Spirit?
Zeal for the temple of God
still consumes Him. (John 2:3-12)

21 January 2016

HOUSE OF MIRRORS

The world– a house of mirrors,
wherein we live and move
and think we get our being from.
Born and raised
in the authority of the image,
projected by distorted mirrors,
in a daze,
we wander around the maze,
seeking the exit.

Away from conflict and
contradiction, we are driven by a
knowing,
a longing for truth and simplicity;
where fragments fit
and missing pieces are found. Where
our mirror,
like a still mountain lake,
reflects an undistorted image:
His.

June 2008

IN HIM

*"In Your light
we see light"
(Psalm 36:9)*

Also true:
in Your Truth
we see truth.

In Your Pain,
we accept pain
and are transformed.

In Your Wisdom,
we are able to discern and
to know wisdom.

In Your Righteousness, we
lay down our own and are
declared righteous.

In Your Holiness,
we are changed
to be more like You.

In Your Love
we come to know love and
become loving.

4 October 2016

IN HIS SAFE KEEPING – AT LAST!

That in-built heart's desire,
familiar to most,
that longing
for a true and lasting soul mate;
my greatest source of pain,
failure, shame and fear.
A dark shadow,
pursuing me.
A hidden snare,
repeatedly tripping me up,
entangling me-
delivering but a poor counterfeit.

Tonight, finally free
from this life-long search!
Surprised at how long it's taken me
to place this sorry saga
into the loving care of Abba Father.
His peace- A sure promise,
in exchange for my anxious striving.
No longer to give it any thought.
Should it once again try to arise,
I will continue reminding myself:
it is now out of my control
and in my loving Father's safe keeping.

29 January 2016

LIFE'S LEARNING

Funny how God,
in his patience,
honours the vows of him
who's never practiced faithfulness before.

Like setting out in a boat,
without having mastered navigation.
Allowing learning to occur on the fly.
I pity his companions!

Foolhardy-
by both navigator
and his crew.
Shipwreck most likely.

That's exactly what we do.
In love, we make our vows-
soon to be broken?
What was that all about?

People are needy,
from birth to the grave.
Character understands,
thinks through and only then commits.

Our God is such.
He ties Himself to us with an unbreakable vow,
knowing full well the state of our hearts.
Because of His heart, safe harbour is assured!

10 July 2010

LIFE'S LINK

Baby asks for it
in its crying.

The young child,
in his tantrums.

The metamorphic teenager,
in his defiance.

The young adult,
in his search for meaning.

The family man,
in his juggling.

The older man,
in his disillusionment.

The old man,
in his search for peace.

"Hesed": an aspect of Agape.
Love, that stems from God.

Fully displayed for us,
in the willing suffering of His Son.

7 July 2010

MIRRORS

In the midst of a noisy carnival,

a maze of mirrors;

all with distortions.

Someone threw a rock-

reflected, a shattered world.

Fragments of differing beliefs;

the illusions of broken people.

Like stalls at universities' open days,

beckoning you to sign up.

The relativity of truth-

where you pick your own version.

Find the one that makes you happy,

from the smörgåsbord of life.

Past heated debating;

eerie laughter echoing

from the master of the carnival.

When ready, step away.

Wander the lonely, deserted streets.

Feel the icy wind

blowing through your very core.

Head towards the desert.

Don't look back.

Throw away your soft drink

and your fairy floss;

only the clouds to distract you now.

Keep going,

for there is a well to be found,

fed by a spring, cool and crystal clear.

The ancient promise of thirst-quenching

water. As you bend down to drink,

you discover a mirror without flaws.

March 1996

MY BELOVED

My Beloved took me for a walk today.
He is an artist, superbly so.
He pointed out to me the endless hues,
the infinite variety of textures
and how He intermingles them.

He is the ultimate landscaper,
displaying expert division of space
into ever-changing sky,
undulating, wooded planes and meadows
and the restless, glistening and sparkling sea.

This, and so much more,
revealing His mind and heart,
overflowing with love to create,
to delight and to bless.
Endowed with perfect insight.

Although, what brought tears to my eyes
wasn't so much the display of His might,
but the heart of my Beloved
Who, although Lord of all,
made Himself Servant of all!

22 March 1984

MY SWITZERLAND

Church bells tolling,
solemnly marking time,
ringing throughout the cities.
Sentinels,
there to remind-
about Carpe Diem?
A national obsession maybe
with managing time?
If sentinels-
they have become
meaningless symbols!
The outward retained,
its truth detained
and locked away.

Nevertheless,
there is an undercurrent
gradually gaining momentum.
A controversial oddity,
a powerful groundswell,
growing in strength
from above.
A hidden chrysalis,
mostly secure in its cocoon,
watched over by Love.
Already though,
the emergence of new creations.
True sentinels,
heralding the wake-up call!

Zürich, Switzerland
12 October 2005

NECESSARY DISILLUSIONMENT

I used to think that the biblical saying
"the heart is desperately wicked"
was at best an exaggeration,
at worst- the description of my own heart.

Lately,
searching for my deeper motives
for seemingly good deeds,
asking for the truth to be revealed.

I soon find
instead of love,
sometimes,
the motive lies in guilt.

Also in insincerity,
inferiority,
in needing to be needed,
to feel good.

What about
to be seen as good,
to prove that I am the strong one?
And the list goes on...

His glory said to dwell in earthen vessels.
As long as I attempt to look good,
to seem loving beyond reproach,
all that is seen is a whitewashed vessel.

Only when that vessel
is allowed to crack and
chip, can the precious
contents finally seep
through.

13 May 2008

NEW WORLD

Are you dreaming of a world
where truth, love and peace
can be trusted?
Where the things
that your heart longs for,
are a rock under your feet
and not quicksand,
as you may be experiencing?

Do you ask yourself,
how can I be loving
and really truthful,
without being taken advantage of
and eaten alive?
You would like to trust,
yet rightly fear
wishful thinking.

From painful experience you know
the world to be hard as nails.
Instead of love- exploitation.
Instead of truth- compromise.
Instead of peace- unceasing striving.
Worse still:
these very things
have now become part of you also.

Torn and tossed between the two;
the wrestle is uneven.
Your dream and hope
for what ought to be-
like a child
wrestling with an adult.
Eventually, some let the child go to sleep,
or forcefully send him to his room.

The One who calls Himself Truth still speaks:
"Seek (and keep on seeking),
and you will find.
Knock, (and keep on knocking),
and the door will be opened onto you." (Matt. 7:7)
This promise stands as dependable
as the rising of the sun each day,
for the One who spoke can be trusted!

Undated (timeless maybe?)

ON MY WAY TO WORK

A day
like any other working day.
Making my way
through the usual city crowd,
in order to get to work.
Then,
out of the blue,
this awesome presence
which seems to envelop me.
A presence
so warm,
so kind,
so reassuring...
Like an embrace
from a loving father,
or what I imagine
a loving father to be like.
He seems to say:
"You belong."
"You are part of Us."
"You are loved and cherished."
I struggle to hold back the tears.
Tears of joy and gratitude!
I've waited all my life to hear those words!
Presently, my smile turns into a grin-
I realize that, for a moment,
I actually forgot where I work!

23 December 2003

OUR MAGNIFICENT DESTINY

How subtly
the enemy moves.
We know it,
yet do we perceive?

Individualism, through ease,
defines how we live and are.
We see it as a fact,
fail to see it as a curse.

Our togetherness-
a weak expression of His love.
Our destiny- to move as one in Him.
Our preconditioned minds- unable to see.

For we do not need each other,
though we say we do.
Keeping ourselves separate,
and therefore living ineffectively.

When dulling ease is far removed,
we may recognize our need of one another.
We then will move together,
to fulfil our magnificent destiny!

12 July 2010

PARADISE

How can we seek after Paradise,
without seeking its Creator and Sustainer?
Yet, we do it all the time!
Each one pursuing,
or attempting to create
our own version of paradise.
The poor seek the paradise of plenty.
The oppressed- freedom and power.
The greedy- wealth and indulgence.
The ugly- beauty that opens doors of favour.
The naive- the false promise of dazzling riches,
simply by finding the right know-how.
The illusion, perpetrated throughout the ages,
of paradise for us alone,
where we will find eternal bliss,
living happily ever after.
A tailor-made lie,
prepared for each one of us,
keeping us busy for a lifetime,
in pursuit of that lost Eden.
Never was there a lie
so effective for generations past
and generations yet to come.
A dangling carrot,
always out of reach.
That shimmering Fata Morgana,
dissolving into the ether,
as soon as you seem to reach it.

I am convinced-
paradise is not a place,
nor a state of being
but rather-
a person:
Jesus Christ His name.
(Ephesians 1:3)

25 February 2016

PRAYER

God of love,
teach me
to continue walking
in love,
continuing to give
and to receive
love.

Especially
when knocked back,
when doors slam closed.
When I bump against
my own limitations and fears,
let me not be like the snail
that retreats in its shell.

God of love,
teach me
to continue walking
in love,
continuing giving
and receiving your Love,
through others.

10 September 1994

PRISONS

Many kinds of prisons;
some made of wood and iron bars
with iron doors and deadbolts,
some within relationships
and the obsessive fear of loss.

The worst kind-
the self-imposed ones.
Those keeping us trapped
in a box labelled "inadequacy",
binding us with cords of shame.

Careful to hide
our real self,
with its brokenness,
its insecurities and failures,
behind a façade of make-belief.

The self-imposed prison door
will freely release its captor-
the key that must be used
is in the shape of a cross,
its name tag: Agape.

19 March 1993

RESTLESS

Chasing time.
Filling void?
Living
according to rules.
Whose?
Failed expectations
or deliberate failure?
Friends with half smiles-
lukewarm?
Unable to give
beyond their ease?
Am I one of them?
Probably, at times!
Impulse buying-
a cupboard full of clothes
not quite matching.
To and fro,
swings the pendulum.
Peace,
only found
when I cease running
from resting in You.

21 June 1994

RISEN

The Prince of Life
chose to wrestle with death;
a battle so fierce,
a conflict so great-
defeat appeared complete.

Like a surfer,
disappearing
under a monster wave.
A boxer,
knocked out in the ring.

Death seemed
to have swallowed him up,
while all of Heaven stood stricken.
The Father,
shedding silent tears.

Yet,
just like the surfer,
rising from under the wave,
the boxer facing another round-
death could not hold Him down!

He is risen,
once and for all!
The Father's tears,
tears of joy and pride
in His victorious Son.

20 November 2007

SCAPEGOAT

The Shepherd of the sheep
heard the lonely cries
of the scapegoat,
driven into the wilderness.
It had been sent there,
carrying other people's sins-
condemned because of them.

He came and rescued me.
Washed me clean of all sins;
theirs and mine, imputed upon me.
Of their judgements,
rejection and condemnation.
Of their decree to dwell in the wilderness
and to roam in arid places.

He has brought me to green pastures
and made me lie near still waters.
He invites me to enjoy His abundance
and to dance amongst the spring lambs.
He has flooded me with His acceptance
and invited me to partake of His Truth-
gradually washing away the lies of the past.

23 November 1996

SEA OF TEARS

Three thirty in the morning
and I'm awake,
in a flood of tears.
The weight of memories,
of irreplaceable losses
and cruel betrayals-
I find myself drowning!

Before this wave of sadness
carries me away,
rudderless,
should I reach for those tablets again?
Get down on my knees
and pray
a prayer of desperation?

I walk to the kitchen
for a comforting drink.
Slowly, becoming conscious
of other struggling lives.
No longer alone now,
I share the sadness and tears
of mankind itself.

This place- a sea of tears,
where broken people
break anew
and are broken by others.
Clinging to fragments
of their shattered dreams,
hoping to be saved from oblivion.

There is a Boatman
and his crew.
Their mission;
to save us from drowning
and to heal our brokenness,
wrapping us in garments of praise
and wiping away every tear (Revelation 21:4).

11 September 2012

SHELTER FROM THE STORM

That cosy cabin,
a shelter from the storm,
could have become
my permanent abode,
had it not been
for a call
to go higher,
to venture out
into the howling tempest,
facing the headwind
and the icy gale.
One last glance back,
shedding a tear of regret.

Then facing onward and upward,
my Faithful Companion
by my side,
to strengthen,
guide
and direct my footsteps,
amidst the mist
and surrounding shrouds of fog.
On treacherous terrain,
till we reach that final destination;
the Palace on High,
where pasture lands abound
and where rivers of life
and calm waters
forever restore the soul.

17 December 2015

SHUTDOWN

In a world,
where man has become
its coincidental final link,
in a purposeless chain of events,
man's thoughts resound
in the draughty corridors of time.
Munchean shadows, screaming,
erratically hastening along,
driven by collective angst,
stooped over by invisible burdens,
searching for existential meaning
and vainly attempting to make sense
of a seemingly senseless universe.

We superimpose bigger telescopes
onto our distorted vision
and fail to perceive the singular,
in relation to the whole.
Shut down the telescopes.
Huddle down in some cave,
out of the gale,
away from all the babble.
Close your eyes
and take a deep breath.
Slowly, a single word will surface;
Help!
And the universe sighs in relief.

Zurich, Switzerland
9 July 1998

SIMPLICITY

Less talk– more silence.
Less things– more time.
Less action– more focus.
Less friends– more friendship.
Less getting– more giving.
Less fear– more trust.
Less of man– more of God.

9 October 1997

SURVIVAL DEMANDS IT

Two ways only
to live on this earth.
The majority-
big fish
eating little ones.
Hunger must be fed.
Needs-
many and varied.
Some- more wants
than needs.

Charm-
to attract,
then entrap.
Spiders,
weaving their webs,
using sources of light
for their own purpose.
Power-
to satisfy the illusion
of control.

"Come onto me..."
the Shepherd calls to the sheep.
Unlike entrepreneurial farmers,
merely throwing bales of hay
into the thronging fold.
Rather,
tenderly and watchfully,
hand-fed,
each one known
by its name.

Sheep,
dwelling peacefully,
harmlessly,
in pastures green
and abundant,
beside the still waters.
Without need
for cunning guile,
in order to thrive
and survive.

4 October 2016

THE ALTAR OF THE LIE

From the womb,
she was trained
and branded
by the dark angel
who guards the prison
of the lonely.

Throughout life,
groomed by abandonment,
betrayal,
abuse and neglect;
tried and tested methods
of recruitment.

Early,
she was taught
to worship at the altar of the lie.
To undergo ceremonial cutting
and to endure continuous bleeding.
Wounds that would not heal.

So far,
many sacrificial offerings:
authentic values in exchange
for superficial relief.
Genuine identity
for others' perception of self.

As for now,
the story could end there
but doesn't.
The prison door
has released its captive.
The healing journey has begun.

The altar-
finally smashed!
Life's ashes,
in exchange for beauty.
Her pain of loneliness
soothed by the balm of trust.

26 June 2005

THE ARTFUL DODGER

During my recent travels,
I met a puzzling group.
Gathering in nobly appointed gardens,
sharing refined cuisine,
conducting thoughtful conversations,
displaying great insight
into the manifold world of knowledge
and exalting those among themselves,
at the forefront of such exchange.
When questioned,
some humbly confessed to deeds,
done and being done
under the banner of charity,
wearing them like a glittering diadem.

In hindsight,
just as prone to his schemes,
I nevertheless could sense
the artful dodger's presence.
Always cleverly disguised
through ceaseless trickery
and clever deception.
His mission:
to promote avoidance of the call,
given by the Master Himself.
The call for the seed to fall to the ground,
and to die,
in order to bear lasting fruit,
useful and pleasing to Him (John 12:24).

17 June 2012

THE DAM

In a vision,
I saw a dam
filled with water.
Sometimes,
the retaining wall would part
and the water would gush forth.
Then,
it would close again
and no water would flow.

I know,
the dam was my heart.
The one operating the dam-
the self, my self,
using my will
and limited understanding,
my emotions,
often triggered
by my circumstances.

I now earnestly desire
to hand over
the control of this dam
to my Lord and friend.
He will open those walls
and leave them permanently so-
allowing the water to flow
unhindered,
as He would want.

11 November 1984

THE FINAL VERDICT

You talk to me of war,
as a yardstick of truth.
You mention the Warsaw ghetto,
the war in Vietnam,
the situation in Palestine,
the present plight in Iraq
and other seemingly senseless events.
You use them to support your beliefs
in man's predominant darkness
and in the universe's journey towards chaos.
All things, you say,
are moving towards destruction.
Death, to you, is the final harvest
of all living things.

You have gathered your evidence,
weighed up the arguments,
and you have made a final verdict.
Will you not stop
and reconsider
re-opening the trial...?
You have presented
only one side of the story.
All these things are true-
darkness is everywhere.
Man's evil ever present.
Due to your chosen world view,
your focus is fixed on evidence
supporting the conclusion you made.

Despite what you and I may believe-
the ultimate verdict,
resounding throughout creation,
has been spoken from above:
*"The light shines in the darkness,
and the darkness did not overcome it."*
(John 1:3)
I venture to add,
this was accomplished
because of another word,
spoken from a cross:
*"Father forgive them,
for they know not what they do."*
(Luke 23:34)

1 August 2004

THE GOLDEN CUP OF POISON

I can feel the consequence
of tasting poison
in that sparkling cup.
My spirit wilting,
curled up in an embryonic state.
My soul mournful,
my body limp,
my mind fluctuating
between ceaseless action
and mindless inertia.
I am hiding away
in my cocoon,
which fails to soothe me,
due to its lapsed due-by-date.

Drawing my attention away
from inner brokenness,
my present state-
that of a self-righteous spinster,
full of jealous disdain
towards those who would tackle life.

20 July 1996

THE GREAT WEDDING FEAST

Before Eden,
the Father dreamed a dream
for His Only Begotten Son.

Just like in Song of Songs,
The Bridegroom
still seeking His bride.

A bride without blemish,
tested in the fire of affliction,
coming forth pure as gold.

His wooing began at a wedding.
It will reach its completion
at the Great Wedding Feast.

The Spirit, the Groom's best man,
has made Himself available
for the Groom's every beck and call.

The invitations are still going out.
The banqueting table is being set.
The bride is being made ready for that day.

November 2011

THE GREATEST GIFT OF ALL

Who doesn't know that Christmas
is a time to give and to receive
marvelous and not so striking gifts?
A time to make peace
with self and our fellow man.
A time to make contact
with those long neglected.
Last but not least,
a time to give out
a little human kindness,
to spread unreserved happiness
and to put a joyous glow
on someone's face.

Yet, year after year,
in very many homes,
the same unobtrusive Gift
remains unopened
and forgotten,
under the Christmas tree.
The Giver,
going through the same sadness,
year after year,
that His Gift has been ignored
or worse; even scorned.
"How could this be?", you may ask.
"Am I doing the same?"

Those gifts,
so central to this Season,
a symbol of the greatest Gift of Love:
a heartbroken Father's giving
of His Only Begotten Son,
in order to redeem His rebellious
and wayward children unto Himself.
By candlelight, we sing the songs,
we pray the prayers,
remembering Him, "Light of the world".
Like children, admiring the gifts under the tree
but never unwrapping His.
This Christmas, maybe?

Undated (sometime in the 80's)

THE IDEALIST

A gift or a curse-
this ability to perceive,
so clearly,
the image, the outline
of the ideal?

The present
jars against that image,
leaving a painful sense of lack
and the compulsion to conform
to the ideal.

This passion- always there!
Like a superimposed grid
or a builder's plumb line;
setting the standard
of the ideal.

There's a need to adjust
two fields of vision
to one single image,
making peace with what is
and the ideal.

The Master Optician
knows the adjustment required.
His vision tenderly embraces
both what is,
as well as His ideal.

23 March 1998

(Interestingly, this poem was written one day before
an appointment with an optician, who diagnosed
me with a "Muscular Eye Convergence Disorder"!)

THE MEANING OF LIFE

The meaning of life...
What life?
Whose life?
What meaning?
Whose meaning?

Isn't life
simply for living?
The meaning-
a quest
beyond our scope?

Why then the abused?
The handicapped?
The rich?
The poor?
And all those at war?

Why this insatiable yearning
for love,
for truth,
for security,
for power?

It is driving us,
mercilessly,
on a seemingly endless quest,
till finally,
we break in despair.

The meaning of life-
so many unanswered questions!
Life reduced to mere existence.
Could its meaning be
that there is meaning!

Undated

(An ageless question?)

THE MYTH OF SELF-SUFFICIENCY

For a while,
I carry on
my usual lifestyle.
Trying to achieve
most of my goals,
the essential ones first.
Then,
gradually arising in me,
emptiness.
I push harder,
ignoring the ache;
the desire for a lover,
some friendly company,
even a cry on someone's shoulder.

Finally,
I sit down,
unsuccessful
in turning a deaf ear
to that insistent plea.
Frustration and helplessness,
anger and guilt ensue,
subsiding to stark perception.
I am not,
as the false self
would like me to believe,
a self-sufficient being
but vulnerable,
due to inner need.

Past attempts
all have fallen short
at stilling the yearning.
A cruel farce?
A sadistic streak
permeating creation?
The reflection
of the character
of its architect?
Presently arising,
a glimmer of understanding.
The wonder and discovery
of purposed dependency
upon a wooing Creator.

April 1992

THE ONE ESSENTIAL THING

(Galatians 2:22)

The one essential thing
required of us,
which demands least action
but is the hardest of all,
is something hardly ever taught.

Instead, our religious selves
never tire listening
to countless methods
of how to improve
and ennoble the self.

We piously pray for more patience,
to overcome our impatient selves.
Or else, we clothe ourselves in sackcloth,
on Mondays, after week-end excess,
resuming the cycle again, Fridays.

We adopt loving mannerisms,
in order to gain favour.
We seek status within our circles
and call it "walking in authority"-
a far cry from the Master's example!

That one essential thing,
without which we simply are deluded,
is the insight and willingness
to consider the striving, religious self
utterly unable to please God.
Unless we recognize the need,
to allow the Spirit to include us in Christ's death,
to daily pick up that cross of death to self,
we will be content to play the religious game-
never knowing the wonder of a resurrected life in Him.

Culburra Beach,
28 January 2016

THE PARABLE OF FIRE

The Teacher's favourite way
to impart spiritual reality
was through parables.
He still speaks through them-
using stones, loaves of bread, or even fire.

Today, I forced my overactive mind
to become still,
while watching dancing flames.
Man and fire;
an ancient and vital partnership!

I noticed some of the wood
starting to smoke-
burned only in part.
When pushed back into the center,
the smoke ceased.

One log even fell out of the fireplace,
as if to emphasize this truth.
Struggling to place it back,
I noticed its glow subside,
causing profuse smoke.

Removed from the center,
without its fire,
it became a mere nuisance.
Even coal, without the flame,
remains just a black piece of char.

20 May 2003

THE RELIGIOUS SELF

I love my spiritual life.
It enhances my demeanour,
refines some of my impulses
and puts me in touch with good people.

Much sharing for me occurring.
I have something to say.
I am heard and valued.
My goals are supported.

Help is given to me
to achieve my dreams.
In turn, I feel generous,
when helping others.

I have something to give
which makes me feel important.
God is giving me abundant life
to enjoy with my family and friends.

I am called blessed by all.
No need for me to struggle.
No need for me to be in pain.
This is His ultimate will for me.

The religious self is all about ME! *(John 3:30)*

16 January 2016

THE TEMPLE

(In memory of the past meditation temple
at Homelands Community, Upper Thora, NSW)

In a secluded place,
with wooded surrounds,
the picturesque Bellinger river nearby-
a graceful yet simple wooden temple,
roofed and open on three sides,
handcrafted mats for comfort.
A place to meditate,
to contemplate the surrounds,
to listen to the singing river,
crickets and birds,
even your own voice!

Thai Chi, taught
and practiced by Roger,
a seeker after spiritual truth.
We had some wonderful talks.
An earnestness about him,
integrity, wholesomeness
and striving after excellence
were expressions of his being.
Strangely,
in his presence
I felt like an awkward child.

He commented once,
disappointed and annoyed,
how little appreciation for the sacred
some visitors seemed to have.
Happy to visit the place,
but not caring to leave it
as they found it.
Instead,
littering with soft drink cans,
cigarette butts and papers;
their unimpressive visiting cards.

That temple, its guardian and visitors
still strike a chord within me,
though part of a different era in my life.
It now represents a sanctuary to me,
spanning across many faiths and philosophies.
A place, symbolizing that primal need in man
to connect with that Great Being
I now call Abba Father.
That process
and the appreciation thereof;
the very thing that sanctifies a temple.

27 November 1990

THE UNIVERSAL FOUNT

I am staying in a van park,
boasting great and majestic trees.
A hill on one side, a lake on the other.
Manicured lawns and flowers everywhere-
a mini-community!
Residents who own their homes-
some, perched right over the lake,
overlooking expansive waters.
Others, backing onto the bush.
Great pride evident everywhere
in one's own little piece of haven.

In the van opposite, an elderly couple,
speaking a foreign tongue.
The man, working outside
nearly all day long,
even in the heat of day.
Small jobs it seems.
At the end of the day,
I cannot tell
what changes he has made.
Occasionally, the woman appears,
hands on hips.

I wish I could go over and ask:
Are you happy here?
Is this how you want to live,
or are you bored?
Maybe not enough to do?
Don't you know that the world
needs people like you?

Not too busy with survival,
nor living up to the Jones.
For who else will care for those
who cannot care for themselves?

Let me tell you about Mary,
sitting all day in a chair– rocking.
Stopped, through locks and restraints,
from wandering off.
Light comes into her eyes
when someone sits down and talks to her,
occasionally patting her hand.
There's Billy, who can't stop stealing.
His friends only pay attention
when he offers to pay.
Standing alone before the sentencing judge.

These are just a few of the people,
all around us.
So many, doing it tough.
Being there for others
taps into the spiritual law
that "it is more blessed to give
than to receive".
Simply, because in giving
we keep open
the fount of receiving,
ensuring that it flows freely.

10 November 2002

TIME ALONE

Time to get away.
I am packing the bare minimum,
ensuring that pen and paper,
and my favourite books
are included,
along with the rest.
What I will wear
does not matter.
I only need to please myself.
Glorious freedom,
just to sit or walk,
to read and write.
No need to talk, except,
like silent breathing,
to the One who always listens,
and to listen
to the One
who always speaks.

December 2004

WAKING FROM STUPOR

How does the world
make sense of faith?
A biased view,
possibly philosophical in nature?
A personal obsession
or a favourite hobby,
indulged in on Sundays,
or when saying table grace?
Spiritual symbolism,
expressed in religious ritual,
stemming from man's existential angst-
a lingering residue of primitive man?
Nothing, to be sure,
assisting or of relevance
with the day to day issues of modern life?
Perception's eccentricities,
best kept private and to oneself?

In order to avoid the ridicule and rancour
of society's imposition of its silent norms,
at times, I have attempted to comply,
out of hunger for acceptance,
or fear of loss of pseudo esteem,
even from sheer battle weariness.
Then, this aching schism arises
and demands a fusion of all parts.
How could I acquiesce and comply
and daily deny this vital part of me?
The very Seal imprinted upon every cell
of the new creation of my being!

I awake from my stupor,
when the pain of denial becomes too great,
only to realize that this kind of suffering
is far greater than the occasional blows
that come from standing out from the rest.

August 1994

To contact author for your feedback or any questions relating to her books or to order further published books, please visit **http://piahorangross.com**

www.ingramcontent.com/pod-product-compliance
Lightning Source LLC
Chambersburg PA
CBHW042345300426
44110CB00030B/166